ULTIMATE POCKET FUN

Knock Knock Jokes

ARCTURUS

ARCTURUS

This edition published in 2019 by Arcturus Publishing Limited
26/27 Bickels Yard, 151–153 Bermondsey Street,
London SE1 3HA

Cover illustration by Adam Clay

ISBN: 978-1-78888-478-5
CH006444NT
Supplier: 08, Date 0619, Print run 9045

Printed in Denmark

Knock, knock...

Who's there?

Cassie.

Cassie who?

Cassie the wood for the trees!

Knock, knock...

Who's there?

Leaf.

Leaf who?

Leaf me alone!

Knock, knock...

Who's there?

Ellie.

Ellie who?

Ellie Funt.

Knock, knock...

Who's there?

Yootha.

Yootha who?

Yootha person with the bicycle for sale?

Knock, knock...

Who's there?

Tessa.

Tessa who?

Tessa long time for you to open the door!

Knock, knock...

Who's there?

Zombie.

Zombie who?

Zombies make honey, others are queens!

Knock, knock...

Who's there?

Ella Man.

Ella Man who?

Ella Man-tary, my dear Watson!

HA!

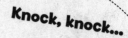

Knock, knock...

Who's there?

Hardy.

Hardy who?

Hardy har, fooled you!

Knock, knock...

Who's there?

Alma.

Alma who?

Alma time seems to be spent on this doorstep!

Knock, knock...

Who's there?

Juicy.

Juicy who?

Juicy what I just saw?

Knock, knock...

Who's there?

Congo.

Congo who?

Congo out, I'm grounded!

Knock, knock...

Who's there?

Who.

Who who?

Is there an owl in there?

Knock, knock...

Who's there?

Alien.

Alien who?

Just how many aliens do you know?

Knock, knock...

Who's there?

Daryl.

Daryl who?

Daryl never be another you!

Knock, knock...

Who's there?

Pizza.

Pizza who?

Pizza on Earth and goodwill to all men!

Knock, knock...

Who's there?

Elsie.

Elsie who?

Elsie you around!

Knock, knock...

Who's there?

Wendy.

Wendy who?

Wendy red, red robin comes bob, bob bobbin' along, along!

Knock, knock...

Who's there?

Bach.

Bach who?

Bach to work, you slackers!

Knock, knock...

Who's there?

You are.

You are who?

I'm not Who, I'm me!

Knock, knock...

Who's there?

Phil.

Phil who?

Phil this bag with money, I'm a robber!

Knock, knock...

Who's there?

Mabel.

Mabel who?

**Mabel doesn't
ring either!**

Knock, knock...

Who's there?

Superman.

Superman who?

**You know I can't reveal
my secret identity!**

Knock, knock...

Who's there?

Phil.

Phil who?

**Phil this cup with sugar please.
I've just run out!**

Knock, knock...

Who's there?

Deanna.

Deanna who?

**Deanna-mals are restless,
open the cage!**

Knock, knock...

Who's there?

Chris.

Chris who?

**Chris P. Bacon, in
time for breakfast!**

Knock, knock...

Who's there?

Conyers.

Conyers who?

Conyers please open the door!

Knock, knock...

Who's there?

Cattle.

Cattle who?

Cattle purr if you stroke it!

Knock, knock...

Who's there?

Jess.

Jess who?

Jess me and my shadow!

Knock, knock...

Who's there?

Zone.

Zone who?

Zone shadow scares him!

Knock, knock...

Who's there?

Canoe.

Canoe who?

Canoe come out and play today?

Knock, knock...

Who's there?

Deena.

Deena who?

Deena hear me the first time?

Knock, knock...

Who's there?

Douglas.

Douglas who?

Douglas is broken!

Knock, knock...

Who's there?

Twitter.

Twitter who?

Have you got an owl in there?

Knock, knock...

Who's there?

Nadia.

Nadia who?

Just Nadia head if you understand what I'm saying!

Knock, knock...

Who's there?

Callista.

Callista who?

Callista warm reception?

Knock, knock...

Who's there?

Russell.

Russell who?

Russell up a nice hot cup of tea—
it's freezing out here!

Knock, knock...

Who's there?

Seymour.

Seymour who?

Seymour of me by opening the door!

Knock, knock...

Who's there?

Zookeeper.

Zookeeper who?

Zookeeper away from him!

Knock, knock...

Who's there?

Cash.

Cash who?

I knew you were nuts!

Knock, knock...

Who's there?

Police.

Police who?

Police let me in, it's freezing out here!

Knock, knock...

Who's there?

Butter.

Butter who?

Butter bring an umbrella, it looks like it might rain!

Knock, knock...

Who's there?

Fangs.

Fangs who?

Fangs for the memory!

Knock, knock...

Who's there?

Glasgow.

Glasgow who?

Glasgow to the movies!

Knock, knock...

Who's there?

Candy.

Candy who?

Candy person who owns this house please open the door!

Knock, knock...

Who's there?

Vince.

Vince who?

Vince some time since I saw you last!

Knock, knock...

Who's there?

Egbert.

Egbert who?

Egbert no bacon!

Knock, knock...

Who's there?

Icing.

Icing who?

Icing carols—you give me money!

Knock, knock...

Who's there?

Anka.

Anka who?

Anka the ship!

Knock, knock...

Who's there?

Madrid.

Madrid who?

Ma-drid you wash my jeans?

Knock, knock...

Who's there?

Dunce.

Dunce who?

Dunce-ay another word!

Knock, knock...

Who's there?

Anita.

Anita who?

Anita borrow a pencil!

Knock, knock...

Who's there?

Aki.

Aki who?

Aki would be really useful right now!

Knock, knock...

Who's there?

Jacklyn.

Jacklyn who?

Jacklyn Hyde!

Knock, knock...

Who's there?

Grant.

Grant who?

Grant you a wish, what is it?

Knock, knock...

Who's there?

Parson.

Parson who?

Parson through and I thought I'd say hello!

Knock, knock...

Who's there?

Ethan.

Ethan who?

Ethan me out of house and home, you are!

Knock, knock...

Who's there?

Belle.

Belle who?

Belle doesn't work, so I'm having to knock!

Knock, knock...

Who's there?

Venice.

Venice who?

Venice this door going to open?

Knock, knock...

Who's there?

Donatello.

Donatello who?

Donatello'n me!

Knock, knock...

Who's there?

Carrie.

Carrie who?

Carrie the bags into the house please!

Knock, knock...

Who's there?

Nuisance.

Nuisance who?

What's nuisance yesterday?

Knock, knock...

Who's there?

Amanda.

Amanda who?

Amanda fix the boiler!

Knock, knock...

Who's there?

A man.

A man who?

A man with a wooden leg.

Tell him to hop it!

Knock, knock...

Who's there?

Leena.

Leena who?

**Leena little closer and
I'll whisper in your ear!**

Knock, knock...

Who's there

Zeb.

Zeb who?

**Zeb better be a good reason for
keeping me waiting out here!**

Knock, knock...

Who's there?

Gopher.

Gopher who?

Gopher broke!

Knock, knock...

Who's there?

Ezra.

Ezra who?

Ezra no hope for me?

Knock, knock...

Who's there?

Jerome.

Jerome who?

Jerome at last!

Knock, knock...

Who's there?

Vassar.

Vassar who?

Vassar girl like you doing in a place like this?

Knock, knock...

Who's there?

Sonia.

Sonia who?

Sonia shoe. I can smell it from here.

Knock, knock...

Who's there?

Jack.

Jack who?

Jackpot! We've won first prize!

Knock, knock...

Who's there?

Munchin.

Munchin who?

**Munchin my dinner and
need a drink.**

Knock, knock...

Who's there?

Gable.

Gable who?

Gable to leap buildings in a single bound!

Knock, knock...

Who's there?

Khan.

Khan who?

Khan you give me a ride to school?

Knock, knock...

Who's there?

CD.

CD who?

CDs fingers? They're freezing—let me in!

Knock, knock...

Who's there?

Disguise.

Disguise who?

Disguise the limit!

Knock, knock...

Who's there?

You.

You who?

You-who to you, too!

Knock, knock...

Who's there?

Edwin.

Edwin who?

Edwin a cup if he could run faster!

Knock, knock...

Who's there?

Chad.

Chad who?

Chad to make your acquaintance!

Knock, knock...

Who's there?

Cora.

Cora who?

Cora wish I had a front door like this!

Knock, knock...

Who's there?

Luck.

Luck who?

**Luck through the keyhole
and you'll find out!**

Knock, knock...

Who's there?

Chimney.

Chimney who?

**Chimney cricket!
Have you seen
Pinocchio?**

Knock, knock...

Who's there?

Mary.

Mary who?

**Mary Christmas,
ho, ho, ho!**

Knock, knock...

Who's there?

Teddy.

Teddy who?

Teddy is the beginning of the rest of your life!

Knock, knock...

Who's there?

Figs.

Figs who?

Figs the doorbell, it's broken!

☆

Knock, knock...

Who's there?

Denis.

Denis who?

Denis anyone?

Knock, knock...

Who's there?

Gorilla.

Gorilla who?

Gorilla cheese sandwich for me and I'll be right over!

Knock, knock...

Who's there?

Otto.

Otto who?

Ottold you two seconds ago!

Knock, knock...

Who's there?

Morse.

Morse who?

Morse come in as quickly as possible!

Knock, knock...

Who's there?

Arch.

Arch who?

Are you catching a cold?

Knock, knock...

Who's there?

Yubin.

Yubin who?

Yubin eating garlic again?

Knock, knock...

Who's there?

Harry.

Harry who?

Harry you been?

Knock, knock...

Who's there?

Alec.

Alec who?

Alec my lollipop!

Knock, knock...

Who's there?

Cohen.

Cohen who?

Cohen to knock just once more, then I'm going away!

Knock, knock...

Who's there?

Brewster.

Brewster who?

Brewster wakes me up every morning singing cock-a-doodle-do!

Knock, knock...

Who's there?

Farmer.

Farmer who?

Farmer distance your house looks much bigger!

Knock, knock...

Who's there?

Misty.

Misty who?

Misty doorbell again!

Knock, knock...

Who's there?

Sherwood.

Sherwood who?

Sherwood like to meet you!

Knock, knock...

Who's there?

Diploma.

Diploma who?

Diploma to fix the leak!

Knock, knock...

Who's there?

Donalette.

Donalette who?

Donalette the bed bugs bite!

43

Knock, knock...

Who's there?

Paul.

Paul who?

Paul up a chair and I'll tell you!

Knock, knock...

Who's there?

Cherry.

Cherry who?

Cherry oh, see you later!

Knock, knock...

Who's there?

Aba.

Aba who?

Aba'out turn. Quick march!

Knock, knock...

Who's there?

Gordy.

Gordy who?

Gordy-rectly to jail, do not pass Go, do not collect da money!

Knock, knock...

Who's there?

Carol.

Carol who?

Carol down the hill, call the police!

Knock, knock...

Who's there?

Greta.

Greta who?

You Greta on my nerves!

HA!

Knock, knock...

Who's there?

Ivan.

Ivan who?

Ivan idea you will know as soon as you open the door!

Knock, knock...

Who's there?

Barry.

Barry who?

Barry the treasure then no one will find it!

Knock, knock...

Who's there?

Argo.

Argo who?

Argo to dance class after school!

Knock, knock...

Who's there?

Theodore.

Theodore who?

Theodore wasn't open so I knocked!

Knock, knock...

Who's there?

Esther.

Esther who?

Esther anything I can do for you?

Knock, knock...

Who's there?

Desi.

Desi who?

Designated hitter!

Knock, knock...

Who's there?

Vera.

Vera who?

Vera long way from home and need a map!

Knock, knock...

Who's there?

Boliva.

Boliva who?

Boliva me, I know what I'm talking about!

Knock, knock...

Who's there?

Police.

Police who?

Police open the door and find out!

Knock, knock...

Who's there?

Gwen.

Gwen who?

Gwen are we going to get together?

Knock, knock...

Who's there?

Willy.

Willy who?

Willy hurry up and let me in!

Knock, knock...

Who's there?

Albee.

Albee who?

Albee a monkey's uncle!

Knock, knock...

Who's there?

Elias.

Elias who?

Elias a terrible thing!

Knock, knock...

Who's there?

Nana.

Nana who?

Nana your business!

Knock, knock...

Who's there?

Ken.

Ken who?

Ken you come out to play?

Knock, knock...

Who's there?

Army.

Army who?

Army aunts coming for dinner?

Knock, knock...

Who's there?

Ivor.

Ivor who?

Ivor sore hand from knocking!

Knock, knock...

Who's there?

Hand.

Hand who?

Hand over your wallet, this is a raid!

Knock, knock...

Who's there?

Jester.

Jester who?

Jester day, you were out. Today, you're in!

Knock, knock...

Who's there?

Constance.

Constance who?

Constance snoring is keeping me awake!

Knock, knock...

Who's there?

Arnie.

Arnie who?

Arnie ever going to let me in?

Knock, knock...

Who's there?

Arf.

Arf who?

Arf full or arf empty!

Knock, knock...

Who's there?

Juno.

Juno who?

Juno the answer?

Knock, knock...

Who's there?

Betty.

Betty who?

Betty earns a lot of money!

Knock, knock...

Who's there?

Ina.

Ina who?

Ina minute I'm going to knock this door down!

Knock, knock...

Who's there?

Chuck.

Chuck who?

Chuck and see if the door is locked!

Knock, knock...

Who's there?

Augusta.

Augusta who?

Augusta wind blew my hat away!!

Knock, knock...

Who's there?

Disk.

Disk who?

Disk is a recorded message, please leave your message after the beep!

Knock, knock...

Who's there?

Butcher.

Butcher who?

Butcher said I could come and visit you!

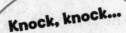

Knock, knock...

Who's there?

Joanna.

Joanna who?

Joanna have a guess?

Knock, knock...

Who's there?

Veal chop.

Veal chop who?

Veal chop around and see vot bargains vee can pick up!

Knock, knock...

Who's there?

Frank.

Frank who?

Frankenstein!

Knock, knock...

Who's there?

Enid.

Enid who?

Enid some more money!

Knock, knock...

Who's there?

Ammonia.

Ammonia who?

Ammonia little kid!

Knock, knock...

Who's there?

Chile.

Chile who?

Chile out tonight, isn't it!

Knock, knock...

Who's there?

Cliff.

Cliff who?

Cliff hanger!

Knock, knock...

Who's there?

Hanover.

Hanover who?

Hanover your money!

Knock, knock...

Who's there?

Major.

Major who?

Major mind up to open the door yet?

Knock, knock...

Who's there?

Lefty.

Lefty who?

Lefty home on your own again!

Knock, knock...

Who's there?

Butter.

Butter who?

Butter open quick, I have to go to the bathroom!

Knock, knock...

Who's there?

Dan.

Dan who?

Dan just stand there—let me in!

Knock, knock...

Who's there?

Don.

Don who?

Don Patrol!

Knock, knock...

Who's there?

Isabelle.

Isabelle who?

Isabelle not a good idea?

Knock, knock...

Who's there? ☆ ☆

Bacon.

Bacon who?

Bacon a cake for your birthday!

Knock, knock...

Who's there?

Goat.

Goat who?

Goat to the door and find out!

Knock, knock...

Who's there?

Insurance salesman.

...

... hello...? hello...?

Knock, knock...

Who's there?

Ben Hur.

Ben Hur who?

Ben Hur an hour—let me in!

Knock, knock...

Who's there?

Sarah.

Sarah who?

**Sarah bell on this door?
I've been knocking for ages!**

Knock, knock...

Who's there?

Arthur.

Arthur who?

Arthur any more cookies in the jar?

Knock, knock...

Who's there?

Reed.

Reed who?

Reed-turn to sender, address unknown!

Knock, knock...

Who's there?

Polly.

Polly who?

Polly door handle again, I think it's just stiff!

Knock, knock...

Who's there?

Aware.

Aware who?

Aware, aware has my little dog gone?

Knock, knock...

Who's there?

Harriet.

Harriet who?

Harriet up!

Knock, knock...

Who's there?

Bill.

Bill who?

Bill-ding's on fire!

Knock, knock...

Who's there?

Mara.

Mara who?

Mara, Mara on the wall!

Knock, knock...

Who's there?

Colin.

Colin who?

Colin the doctor, I feel ill!

Knock, knock...

Who's there?

Avon.

Avon who?

Avon to drink your blood!

Knock, knock...

Who's there?

Lucretia.

Lucretia who?

Lucretia from the Black Lagoon!

Knock, knock...

Who's there?

Honor Claire.

Honor Claire who?

Honor Claire day, you can see forever!

Knock, knock...

Who's there?

Cecile.

Cecile who?

**Cecile th-the windows.
Th-there's a m-monster out there.**

Knock, knock...

Who's there?

Aardvark.

Aardvark who?

**Aardvark a million
miles for one of your
smiles!**

Knock, knock...

Who's there?

Anthem.

Anthem who?

Anthem prince seeking pretty princess.

Knock, knock...

Who's there?

Gin.

Gin who?

Gin know how cold it is out here?

Knock, knock...

Who's there?

Ahab.

Ahab who?

Ahab to go to the bathroom. Quick, open the door!

Knock, knock...

Who's there?

Ivory.

Ivory who?

Ivory strong, just like Tarzan!

Knock, knock...

Who's there?

Yul.

Yul who?

Yul soon see!

Knock, knock...

Who's there?

Chopin.

Chopin who?

Chopin in the supermarket.

LOL

Knock, knock...

Who's there?

Apple.

Apple who?

Apple your hair if you don't let me in!

Knock, knock...

Who's there?

Elvis.

Elvis who?

Elvis is a complete waste of time, I'm off!

Knock, knock...

Who's there?

Jackson.

Jackson who?

Jackson the telephone, do you want to talk to him?

Knock, knock...

Who's there?

Our Tell.

Our Tell who?

Our Tell you what I want, what I really really want!

74

Knock, knock...

Who's there?

Ella.

Ella who?

Ella-vator. Doesn't that give you a lift?

Knock, knock...

Who's there?

Anna.

Anna who?

Anna gonna tell you!

Knock, knock...

Who's there?

Betty.

Betty who?

Betty ya don't know who this is!

Knock, knock...

Who's there?

Mike.

Mike who?

Mike your mind up!

Knock, knock...

Who's there?

Carlo.

Carlo who?

Carload of junk!

Knock, knock...

Who's there?

Freighter.

Freighter who?

I'm Freighter open the door!

Knock, knock...

Who's there?

Galway.

Galway who?

Galway, you're annoying me!

Knock, knock...

Who's there?

Oliver.

Oliver who?

Oliver cross the road from you!

Knock, knock...

Who's there?

Ya.

Ya who?

What are you getting so excited about?

Knock, knock...

Who's there?

Fletch.

Fletch who?

Fletch a bucket of water, your house is on fire!

Knock, knock...

Who's there?

Cole.

Cole who?

Cole as a cucumber!

Knock, knock...

Who's there?

Ferdie.

Ferdie who?

Ferdie last time, open this door!

Knock, knock...

Who's there?

Spider.

Spider who?

Spider what everyone says, I like you!

Knock, knock...

Who's there?

Björn.

Björn who?

Björn to be wild!

Knock, knock...

Who's there?

Mandy.

Mandy who?

Mandy lifeboats!

Knock, knock...

Who's there?

Arnold.

Arnold who?

Arnold friend you haven't seen for years!

Knock, knock...

Who's there?

Icon.

Icon who?

**Icon tell you another knock, knock
joke if you want me to!**

Knock, knock...

Who's there?

Kari.

Kari who?

**Kari on like this and I'll freeze to
death out here!**

Knock, knock...

Who's there?

Dot.

Dot who?

Dots for me to know, and you to find out.

Knock, knock...

Who's there?

Igloo.

Igloo who?

Igloo knew Suzie like I know Suzie!

Knock, knock...

Who's there?

Anita.

Anita who?

Anita you like I need a hole in the head!

⭐ ⭐

Knock, knock...

Who's there?

Atlas.

Atlas who?

Atlas it's the weekend!

Knock, knock...

Who's there?

Gandhi.

Gandhi who?

Gandhi cane!

Knock, knock...

Who's there?

Dime.

Dime who?

Dime to tell another knock, knock joke!

Knock, knock...

Who's there?

Cargo.

Cargo who?

Cargo beep! beep!

Knock, knock...

Who's there?

Aries.

Aries who?

Aries a reason I'm knocking at your door!

Knock, knock...

Who's there?

Candy.

Candy who?

Candy owner of this big red car come and move it off my driveway!

Knock, knock...

Who's there?

Alpaca.

Alpaca who?

Alpaca the trunk, you packa the suitcase!

Knock, knock...

Who's there?

Accordion.

Accordion who?

HA!

Accordion to the weather forecast, it's going to rain tomorrow!

Knock, knock...

Who's there?

Island.

Island who?

Island on your roof with my parachute!

Knock, knock...

Who's there?

Izzy.

Izzy who?

Izzy come, Izzy go!

Knock, knock...

Who's there?

Olivia.

Olivia who?

Olivia, so get out of my house!

Knock, knock...

Who's there?

Congo.

Congo who?

Congo into the woods, it's dangerous!

Knock, knock...

Who's there?

Omar.

Omar who?

Omar goodness gracious, wrong door!

Knock, knock...

Who's there?

Yah.

Yah who?

Yahoo! Ride'em, cowboy!

Knock, knock...

Who's there?

Diesel.

Diesel who?

Diesel make you feel better!

Knock, knock...

Who's there?

Ben.

Ben who?

Ben wondering what you're up to!

Knock, knock...

Who's there?

Germany.

Germany who?

Germany people knock on your door?

Knock, knock...

Who's there?

Butcher.

Butcher who?

Butcher didn't know it was me at the door, did you?

Knock, knock...

Who's there?

Moo.

Moo who?

Well, make up your mind, are you a cow or an owl?

Knock, knock...

Who's there?

Telly.

Telly who?

Telly your friend to come out!

Knock, knock...

Who's there?

Patrick.

Patrick who?

Patricked me into knocking on your door!

Knock, knock...

Who's there?

Amish.

Amish who?

Amish you too!

Knock, knock...

Who's there?

Oink moo.

Oink moo who?

You are confused, aren't you?!

Knock, knock...

Who's there?

Handel.

Handel who?

Handel with care!

Knock, knock...

Who's there?

Jaws.

Jaws who?

Jaws truly!

Knock, knock...

Who's there?

Turner.

Turner who?

Turner round, there's a monster behind you!

Knock, knock...

Who's there?

Argue.

Argue who?

Argue going to let me in or not???

Knock, knock...

Who's there?

Rabbit.

Rabbit who?

Rabbit up carefully, it's a present!

Knock, knock...

Who's there?

Buddha.

Buddha who?

Buddha this slice of bread for me!

Knock, knock...

Who's there?

Haydn.

Haydn who?

Haydn in this cupboard is boring!

Knock, knock...

Who's there?

Custer.

Custer who?

Custer lot to find out!

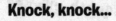

Knock, knock...

Who's there?

Snow.

Snow who?

Snow use, I've lost my key again!

Knock, knock...

Who's there?

Andrew.

Andrew who?

Andrew a picture!

Knock, knock...

Who's there?

Butternut.

Butternut who?

Butternut squash the eggs!

Knock, knock...

Who's there?

Soup.

Soup who?

Souperman!

HA!

Knock, knock...

Who's there?

Kay.

Kay who?

Kay, L, M, N, O, P, Q, R, S, T, U, V, W, X, y, Z!

Knock, knock...

Who's there?

Mike.

Mike who?

Mike car won't start, can I come in and use the phone?

Knock, knock...

Who's there?

Hans.

Hans who?

Hans off the table!

Knock, knock...

Who's there?

Yodel.

Yodel who?

**Yodel who to you too!
Let's form a yodelling duo!**

Knock, knock...

Who's there?

Amy.

Amy who?

Amy fraid I've forgotten!

Knock, knock...

Who's there?

Hank.

Hank who?

Hank you!

Knock, knock...

Who's there?

Dublin.

Dublin who?

Dublin up with laughter!

Knock, knock...

Who's there?

Ginger.

Ginger who?

Ginger hear the doorbell?

Knock, knock...

Who's there?

Aretha.

Aretha who?

Aretha holly on your door.

Knock, knock...

Who's there?

Yvette.

Yvette who?

Yvette helps lots of animals.

Knock, knock...

Who's there?

Josie.

Josie who?

Josie any reason to keep me waiting out here?

Knock, knock...

Who's there?

Scott.

Scott who?

Scott nothing to do with you!

Knock, knock...

Who's there?

A little girl.

A little girl who?

A little girl who can't reach the doorbell!

Knock, knock...

Who's there?

Henrietta.

Henrietta who?

Henrietta toadstool, but thought it was a mushroom!

Knock, knock...

Who's there?

LOL

Phyllis.

Phyllis who?

Phyllis bucket with water, please!

Knock, knock...

Who's there?

Amanda.

Amanda who?

Amanda the table!

Knock, knock...

Who's there?

Omelet.

Omelet who?

Omelet smarter than I look!

Knock, knock...

Who's there?

Eyesore.

Eyesore who?

Eyesore do like you!

Knock, knock...

Who's there?

Desiree.

Desiree who?

Desiree of
sunshine in my life!

Knock, knock...

Who's there?

Rita.

Rita who?

**Rita book, you might
learn something!**

Knock, knock...

Who's there?

Dwayne.

Dwayne who?

Dwayne the bathtub, it's overflowing!

Knock, knock...

Who's there?

Beezer.

Beezer who?

Beezer black and yellow and make honey!

Knock, knock...

Who's there?

Aaron.

Aaron who?

Aaron the side of caution!

Knock, knock...

Who's there?

Costas.

Costas who?

Costas a fortune to get here!

Knock, knock...

Who's there?

Jess.

Jess who?

I give up, who?

Knock, knock...

Who's there?

Harold.

Harold who?

Harold are you?

Knock, knock...

Who's there?

Tuna.

Tuna who?

Tuna whole orchestra!

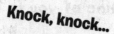

Knock, knock...

Who's there?

Ben.

Ben who?

Ben knocking on this door all morning!

Knock, knock...

Who's there?

Kline.

Kline who?

Kline of you to invite me round!

Knock, knock...

Who's there?

Sarah.

Sarah who?

Sarah phone I can use?

Knock, knock...

Who's there?

Thumping.

Thumping who?

Thumping green and slimy is crawling up your back!

Knock, knock...

Who's there?

Element.

Element who?

Element to tell you that she can't see you today!

Knock, knock...

Who's there?

Atilla.

Atilla who?

Atilla you open this door I'm a gonna stand here!

Knock, knock...

Who's there?

Lionel.

Lionel who?

Lionel bite you if you put your head in its mouth!!!

Knock, knock...

Who's there?

Althea.

Althea who?

Althea later, alligator!

Knock, knock...

Who's there?

Water.

Water who?

Water you doing in my house?

Knock, knock...

Who's there?

Dale.

Dale who?

Dale come if you ask dem!

Knock, knock...

Who's there?

Allied.

Allied who?

Allied, so sue me!

Knock, knock...

Who's there?

Cereal.

Cereal who?

Cereal pleasure to meet you!

Knock, knock...

Who's there?

Andy.

Andy who?

Andy mosquito bit me again!

Knock, knock...

Who's there?

Sid.

Sid who?

Sid you'd be ready by three—where are you?!

Knock, knock...

Who's there?

Indy.

Indy who?

Indy hallway is some of my stuff, and I've come to collect it!

Knock, knock...

Who's there?

Diana.

Diana who?

Diana of thirst. Can I have a glass of water please?

Knock, knock...

Who's there?

Chuck.

Chuck who?

Chuck the key under the door and I'll let myself in!

Knock, knock...

Who's there?

Beethoven.

Beethoven who?

Beethoven is too hot!

Knock, knock...

Who's there?

Max.

Max who?

Max no difference!

Knock, knock...

Who's there?

Adolf.

Adolf who?

Adolf ball hit me in de mouf!

HA!

Knock, knock...

Who's there?

Deduct.

Deduct who?

Donald Deduct!

Knock, knock...

Who's there?

Bean.

Bean who?

Bean fishing lately?

Knock, knock...

Who's there?

Eileen.

Eileen who?

Eileen down to tie my shoe!

Knock, knock...

Who's there?

Alfie.

Alfie who?

Alfie terrible if you leave!

Knock, knock...

Who's there?

Carl.

Carl who?

Carl get you there quicker than if you walk!

Knock, knock...

Who's there?

Dill.

Dill who?

Dill we meet again!

Knock, knock...

Who's there?

Posh.

Posh who?

Posh the door open and you'll see!

Knock, knock...

Who's there?

Carmen.

Carmen who?

Carmen get it!

Knock, knock...

Who's there?

Haden.

Haden who?

Haden seek!

Knock, knock...

Who's there?

Alva.

Alva who?

Alva heart!

Knock, knock...

Who's there?

Cow-go.

Cow-go who?

No, cow go MOO!!!

Knock, knock...

Who's there?

Zany.

Zany who?

Zany body home?

Knock, knock...

Who's there?

Oman.

Oman who?

Oman, you are cute!

Knock, knock...

Who's there?

Luke.

Luke who?

Luke through the keyhole and you'll see!

Knock, knock...

Who's there?

Guess Simon.

Guess Simon who?

Guess Simon the wrong doorstep!

Knock, knock...

Who's there?

Carla.

Carla who?

Carla taxi, I'm leaving!

Knock, knock...

Who's there?

Eva.

Eva who?

Eva you're deaf or your doorbell isn't working!

Knock, knock...

Who's there?

Belize.

Belize who?

Belize in yourself!

Knock, knock...

Who's there?

Hawaii.

Hawaii who?

I'm fine, Hawaii you?

Knock, knock...

Who's there?

Amahl.

Amahl who?

Amahl shook up!

Knock, knock...

Who's there?

Candace.

Candace who?

Candace be true?

Knock, knock...

Who's there?

Yogurt.

Yogurt who?

Yogurt to love my jokes!

Knock, knock...

Who's there?

Cathy.

Cathy who?

Cathy the doorbell, it's too dark out here!

Knock, knock...

Who's there?

Theodore.

Theodore who?

Theodore is stuck and it won't open!

Knock, knock...

Who's there?

Alaska.

Alaska who?

**Alaska again, please
open the door!**

Knock, knock...

Who's there?

Giraffe.

Giraffe who?

Giraffe to ask me that stupid question?

Knock, knock...

Who's there?

Brigham.

Brigham who?

Brigham back my sunshine to me!

HA!

Knock, knock...

Who's there?

May.

May who?

May the force be with you!

Knock, knock...

Who's there?

Cynthia.

Cynthia who?

Cynthia been away I've missed you!

Knock, knock...

Who's there?

I-8.

I-8 who?

I-8 lunch already... When is dinner?

Knock, knock...

Who's there?

Aunt Lou.

Aunt Lou who?

Aunt Lou do you think you are?

Knock, knock...

Who's there?

Curry.

Curry who?

Curry me back home will you?

Knock, knock...

Who's there?

Little old lady.

Little old lady who?

Your yodeling's getting much better!

Knock, knock...

Who's there?

Ivan.

Ivan who?

Ivan infectious disease, so watch out!

Knock, knock...

Who's there?

Waiter.

Waiter who?

Waiter minute, this isn't my house!

Knock, knock...

Who's there?

Wanda.

Wanda who?

Wanda know how much longer you're going to keep me hanging around out here!

Knock, knock...

Who's there?

Waddle.

Waddle who?

Waddle you give me if I promise to go away?

Knock, knock...

Who's there?

Alfalfa.

Alfalfa who?

Alfalfa you, if you give me a kiss!

Knock, knock...

Who's there?

Perth.

Perth who?

Perth your lips and whistle!

Knock, knock...

Who's there?

Ethan.

Ethan who?

Ethan too much makes you fat!

Knock, knock...

Who's there?

Rufus.

Rufus who?

Rufus on fire!

Knock, knock...

Who's there?

Edith.

Edith who?

Edith, it'll make you feel better!

Knock, knock...

Who's there?

McKee.

McKee who?

McKee doesn't fit!

Knock, knock...

Who's there?

Chris.

Chris who?

Christmas is coming and the goose is getting fat!

LOL

Knock, knock...

Who's there?

Berlin.

Berlin who?

Berlin the water for my hard—boiled eggs!

Knock, knock...

Who's there?

Bernadette.

Bernadette who?

Bernadette all my dinner and now I'm starving!

Knock, knock...

Who's there?

The Vampire.

The Vampire who?

The Vampire State Building!

Knock, knock...

Who's there?

Genoa.

Genoa who?

Genoa any new jokes?

Knock, knock...

Who's there?

Ferrer.

Ferrer who?

Ferrer'vrything there is a season!

Knock, knock...

Who's there?

Snow.

Snow who?

Snow use—I can't remember!

Knock, knock...

Who's there?

Amory.

Amory who?

Amory Christmas!

Knock, knock...

Who's there?

Dragon.

Dragon who?

Dragon your feet again!

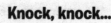

Knock, knock...

Who's there?

Barbara.

Barbara who?

Barbara black sheep!

Knock, knock...

Who's there?

Henrietta.

Henrietta who?

Henrietta worm that was in his apple!

Knock, knock...

Who's there?

Ivor.

Ivor who?

Ivor good mind not to tell you now!

Knock, knock...

Who's there?

Harry.

Harry who?

Harry up! There's a monster behind us!

Knock, knock...

Who's there?

Baby.

Baby who?

Baby I shouldn't hab come round wiv dis cold!

Knock, knock...

Who's there?

Queen.

Queen who?

Queen as a whistle!

Knock, knock...

Who's there?

Jez.

Jez who?

Jez me, that's who!

Knock, knock...

Who's there?

Avenue.

Avenue who?

Avenue guessed yet?

Knock, knock...

Who's there?

Fresno.

Fresno who?

Rudolf the Fresno reindeer!

Knock, knock...

Who's there?

Turkey.

Turkey who?

Turkey and find out!

Knock, knock...

Who's there?

Emma.

Emma who?

Emma bit cold out here, can you let me in?

Knock, knock...

Who's there?

Cass.

Cass who?

Cass more flies with honey than vinegar!

Knock, knock...

Who's there?

Ear.

Ear who?

Ear you are! I've been looking for you!

Knock, knock...

Who's there?

Jools.

Jools who?

**Jools like these
should be worth a
lot of money!**

Knock, knock...

Who's there?

Postman Pat.

Have you got a parcel?

**No, but I've got a black
and white cat!**

Knock, knock...

Who's there?

Champ.

Champ who?

Champ-oo in my eyes. I can't see!

Knock, knock...

Who's there?

Eddie.

Eddie who?

Eddie body home?

Knock, knock...

Who's there?

Jim.

Jim who?

Jim mind if I stay here tonight?

Knock, knock...

Who's there?

Eugene.

Eugene who?

Eugene, me Tarzan!

Knock, knock...

Who's there?

Larva.

Larva who?

Larva cup of coffee.

Knock, knock...

Who's there?

Dad.

Dad who?

Dad fuel to the fire!

Knock, knock...

Who's there?

Earl.

Earl who?

Earl be glad to tell you when you open this door!

Knock, knock...

Who's there?

Josie.

Josie who?

Josie anyone else out here?

Knock, knock...

Who's there?

Topic.

Topic who?

Topic a wild flower is against the law!

Knock, knock...

Who's there?

Willy.

Willy who?

Willy lend me a street map? I'm a stranger in town!

Knock, knock...

Who's there?

Rosie.

Rosie who?

Rosie cheeks!

Knock, knock...

Who's there?

Butter.

Butter who?

Butter let me in!

Knock, knock...

Who's there?

Howl.

Howl who?

Howl you know unless you open the door?

Knock, knock...

Who's there?

Violet.

Violet who?

Violet the cat out of the bag!

Knock, knock...

Who's there?

Steve.

Steve who?

Steve upper lip!

Knock, knock...

Who's there?

Eeyore.

Eeyore who?

Eeyore-ways keeps me waiting!

Knock, knock...

Who's there?

Don.

Don who?

Don be afraid... look into my eyes... you are feeling sleepy...

Knock, knock...

Who's there?

Mae.

Mae who?

Mae be I'll tell you or maybe I won't!

Knock, knock...

Who's there?

Axl.

Axl who?

Axl me nicely and I might just tell you!

Knock, knock...

Who's there?

Eamonn.

Eamonn who?

Eamonn a good mood today, can I come in?

Knock, knock...

Who's there?

Hedda.

Hedda who?

Hedda Nuff! I'm bored of waiting!

Knock, knock...

Who's there?

Felix.

Felix who?

Felix my ice cream, I'll lick his!

Knock, knock...

Who's there?

Amos.

Amos who?

Amosquito just bit me!

Knock, knock...

Who's there?

Cam.

Cam who?

Camelot is where King Arthur lived!

Knock, knock...

Who's there?

De Niro.

De Niro who?

**De Niro I am to you,
the more I like you!**

Knock, knock...

Who's there?

Olive.

Olive who?

Olive right next door to you!

Knock, knock...

Who's there?

Paul.

Paul who?

Paul the other one, it's got bells on!

Knock, Knock...

Who's there?

Shelby.

Shelby who?

Shelby coming round the mountain when she comes!

Knock, knock...

Who's there?

Sally.

Sally who?

Sally-brate the best moments of your life!

Knock, knock...

Who's there?

Chicken.

Chicken who?

Chicken the oven, I can smell burning!

Knock, knock...

Who's there?

Lauren.

Lauren who?

Lauren order!

Knock, knock...

Who's there?

Havanna.

Havanna who?

Havanna wonderful time, wish you were here!

Knock, knock...

Who's there?

Wooden shoe.

Wooden shoe who?

Wooden shoe like to hear another joke?

Knock, knock...

Who's there?

Cheese.

Cheese who?

Cheese a cute dog!

Knock, knock...

Who's there?

Olive.

Olive who?

Olive you!

Knock, knock...

Who's there?

Kent.

Kent who?

Kent you tell by my voice?

Knock, knock...

Who's there?

Pearce.

Pearce who?

Pearce this balloon with a pin!

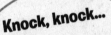

Knock, knock...

Who's there?

Darwin.

Darwin who?

I'll be Darwin you open the door!

Knock, knock...

Who's there?

Lisbon.

Lisbon who?

Lisbon to see me, now she's come to see you!

Knock, knock...

Who's there?

Wade.

Wade who?

Wade down upon the Swanee River!

Knock, knock...

Who's there?

Ike.

Ike who?

Ike can't stop laughing!

Knock, knock...

Who's there?

Hannah.

Hannah who?

Hannah partridge in a pear tree!

Knock, knock...

Who's there?

Boo.

Boo who?

Don't get upset, it's only a game!

Knock, knock...

Who's there?

Ice cream.

Ice cream who?

Ice cream every time I see a ghost!

Knock, knock...

Who's there?

Hugo.

Hugo who?

Hugo your way and I'll go mine!

Knock, knock...

Who's there?

Rhoda.

Rhoda who?

Row, Row, Rhoda boat!

Knock, knock...

Who's there?

Wendy.

Wendy who?

Wendy you want me to call round again?

Knock, knock...

Who's there?

C-2.

C-2 who?

C-2 it that you don't forget my name next time!

Knock, knock...

Who's there?

Mary Lee.

Mary Lee who?

**Mary Lee, Mary Lee,
life is but a dream!
Row, row...**

Knock, knock...

Who's there?

Toffee.

Toffee who?

**Toffee loved is the best
feeling in the world!**

Knock, knock...

Who's there?

Scold.

Scold who?

Scold outside.

Knock, knock...

Who's there?

Daisy.

Daisy who?

Daisy plays, nights he sleeps!

Knock, knock...

Who's there?

Hammond.

Hammond who?

Hammond eggs for breakfast.

Knock, knock...

Who's there?

U-8.

U-8 who?

U-8 my lunch!

Knock, knock...

Who's there?

Heidi.

Heidi who?

Heidi-clare war on you!

Knock, knock...

Who's there?

Sam.

Sam who?

Sam-enchanted evening!

Knock, knock...

Who's there?

Just Paul.

Just Paul who?

**Just Pauling your leg—
it's Steve really!**

Knock, knock...

Who's there?

Isadore.

Isadore who?

**Isadore on the right
way round?**

Knock, knock...

Who's there?

Banana.

Banana who?

Knock, knock...

Who's there?

Banana.

Banana who?

Knock, knock...

Who's there?

Orange.

Orange who?

Orange you glad I didn't say banana?

Knock, knock...

Who's there?

Havelock.
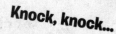

Havelock who?

Havelock put on your door!

Knock, knock...

Who's there?

Harmon.

Harmon who?

Harmon your side!

Knock, knock...

Who's there?

Aida.

Aida who?

Aida lot of chocolates and now I've got tummy ache!

Knock, knock...

Who's there?

Iona.

Iona who?

Iona have eyes for you!

Knock, knock...

Who's there?

Zeke.

Zeke who?

Zeke and you will find!

Knock, knock...

Who's there?

Yachts.

Yachts who?

Yachts up, doc?!?

Knock, knock...

Who's there?

Sacha.

Sacha who?

Sacha fuss over nothing!

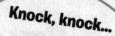

Knock, knock...

Who's there?

Adair.

Adair who?

Adair once, but I'm bald now!

Knock, knock...

Who's there?

Dexter.

Dexter who?

Dexter halls with boughs of holly.

Knock, knock...

Who's there?

Carol.

Carol who?

Carol go if you switch the ignition on!

Knock, knock...

Who's there?

Julia.

Julia who?

Julia want some milk and cookies?

Knock, knock...

Who's there?

Pat.

Pat who?

Pat yourself on the back!

Knock, knock...

Who's there?

Alex.

Alex who?

Alex the questions round here!

Knock, knock...

Who's there?

Dakota.

Dakota who?

Dakota is too small!

Knock, knock...

Who's there?

Cy.

Cy who?

Cy'n on the dotted line!

Knock, knock...

Who's there?

Derek.

Derek who?

Derek get richer and de poor get poorer!

Knock, knock...

Who's there?

Red.

Red who?

Red your letters, you can have them back now!

Knock, knock...

Who's there?

Howard.

Howard who?

Howard is it to recognize my voice? I'm your best friend!

Knock, knock...

Who's there?

Abba, Abba.

Abba, Abba who?

Abba Merry Christmas and Abba Happy New Year!

Knock, knock...

Who's there?

Closure.

Closure who?

Closure mouth when you're eating!

Knock, knock...

Who's there?

Abbey.

Abbey who?

Abbey stung me on the nose!

Knock, knock...

Who's there?

Fonda.

Fonda who?

Fonda you!

Knock, knock...

Who's there?

Tom Sawyer.

Tom Sawyer who?

Tom Sawyer underwear!

Knock, knock...

Who's there?

Gopher.

Gopher who?

Gopher help, I'm stuck in the mud!

Knock, knock...

Who's there?

Alison.

Alison who?

Alison at the keyhole sometimes!

Knock, knock...

Who's there?

Guthrie.

Guthrie who?

Guthrie blind mice!

Knock, knock...

Who's there?

Thayer.

Thayer who?

Thayer thorry or I'll throw thith pie in your face!

Knock, knock...

Who's there?

Handsome.

Handsome who?

Handsome money through the keyhole and I'll tell you more!

Knock, knock...

Who's there?

Scott.

Scott who?

**Scott a creepy look about it, this place.
I think it's haunted!**

Knock, knock...

Who's there?

Teacher.

Teacher who?

Teacher self for a few days. I'm having a break!

Knock, knock...

Who's there?

Ford.

Ford who?

Ford he's a jolly good fellow!

Knock, knock...

Who's there?

Ben.

Ben who?

Knock, knock...

Who's there?

Jester.

Jester who?

Ben down and tie your shoelaces!

Jester minute, I'm trying to find my keys!

Knock, knock...

Who's there?

Esau.

Esau who?

Esau you in the bath!

Knock, knock...

Who's there?

Despair.

Despair who?

Despair room is full of junk!

Knock, knock...

Who's there?

Cello.

Cello who?

Cello, how are you?

Knock, knock...

Who's there?

Wendy.

Wendy who?

Wendy wind blows de cradle will rock.

Knock, knock...

Who's there?

Darren.

Darren who?

Darren people in their flying machines!

Knock, knock...

Who's there?

Nobel.

Nobel who?

Nobel, that's why I knocked!

Knock, knock...

Who's there?

Norma Lee.

Norma Lee who?

Norma Lee I don't go around knocking on doors, but do you want to buy a set of encyclopedias?

Knock, knock...

Who's there?

Hippo.

Hippo who?

Hippo-hop, dance till I drop!

Knock, knock...

Who's there?

Delhi.

Delhi who?

Delhicatessen!

Knock, knock...

Who's there?

Carmen.

Carmen who?

Carmen like best is a Ferrari!

Knock, knock...

Who's there?

Batman.

Batman who?

You mean there's more than one?!

Knock, knock...

Who's there?

Tank.

Tank who?

You're welcome!

Knock, knock...

Who's there?

Muffin.

Muffin who?

Muffin the matter with me. How about you?

Knock, knock...

Who's there?

Karl.

Karl who?

I'll Karl again another day when you're feeling better!

Knock, knock...

Who's there?

Brad.

Brad who?

Brad news, I'm afraid – this is the last knock, knock joke!

HA!

Knock, knock...

Who's there?

Duck.

Duck who?

Just duck—they're throwing things at us!

Knock, knock...

Who's there?

Boo.

Boo who?

Bootiful front door you have.

Knock, knock...

Who's there?

Blue.

Blue who?

Blue away with the wind!

Knock, knock...

Who's there?

Toby.

Toby who?

Toby or not to be!

Knock, knock...

Who's there?

Tex.

Tex who?

Tex you ages to open the door!

Knock, knock...

Who's there?

Lettuce.

Lettuce who?

Lettuce in and you will find out!

Knock, knock...

Who's there?

Peg.

Peg who?

Peg your pardon, I've got the wrong door!

Knock, knock...

Who's there?

Caesar.

Caesar who?

Caesar jolly good fellow!

Knock, knock...

Who's there?

Sam.

Sam who?

Sam person who knocked on the door last time!

Knock, knock...

Who's there?

Homer.

Homer who?

Homer goodness! I can't remember my name!

Knock, knock...

Who's there?

Linda.

Linda who?

Linda hand to get this heavy suitcase up the steps!

Knock, knock...

Who's there?

Howard.

 Howard who?

Howard you know if you won't even open the door?

Knock, knock...

Who's there?

Pasture.

Pasture who?

Pasture bedtime, isn't it?

Knock, knock...

Who's there?

Alec.

Alec who?

Alec-tricity. Isn't that a shock?

Knock, knock...

Who's there?

Thermos.

Thermos who?

Thermos be a better knock, knock joke than this!

Knock, knock...

Who's there?

Lion.

Lion who?

Lion down on the job again!

Knock, knock...

Who's there?

Wood.

Wood who?

Wood you like to let me in now?

Knock, knock...

Who's there?

Dishes.

Dishes who?

Dishes the police! Open up!